LEAVE THE INSANITY BEHIND

LEAVE THE
INSANITY BEHIND

Teacher

CHANNELED BY MIRIANDRA ROTA

Published by Visionary Works Publishing

I have come forth to speak this teaching to you, for you. I am reaching out the hand of love, offering you a rescue, a rescue from succumbing to despair over what resides in the battle, in the suffering.

I am offering you a hand of love and if you dare to take it, you can discover a new freedom and the freedom will give you a way to love, to care and still be free from that aching heart over the suffering of the masses.

-Teacher

DEDICATION

For Teacher, a Spirit Being who is always ready to help us, guide us in every possible way. Thank you.

Perhaps you feel that something, you don't know what, is missing? You have tried all of the ways to do your best. I have seen that. You have given and you have learned how to discern truth from untruth. Yet. Yes, there is that yet. I am here to tell you that one of the primary reasons that you seem to be still unfulfilled within your entire being is that there is a great occurrence upon the earth... and it is not going to go away any time soon.

- Teacher

CONTENTS

INTRODUCTION

These words are spoken for those who live upon earth. It is most likely that you have felt as if there is an insanity occurring upon the earth, that there are leaders who are seeming to be insane, that there are decisions that seem to be insane, and that there are conditions that are horrific...and no one seems to care. No one seems to care that there are thousands and thousands of lives taken daily upon this earth and no one knows...simply because there are causes and effects that require their attention...and the rest continues to occur. Do you see?

Even if you haven't thought in those terms, I, Teacher, am here to tell you, to alert you that you either directly or indirectly are being affected by what is occurring upon this great earth of yours.

And I am here to speak with you and to deliver into your hands ways that will help you remain clear of the insanity.

It does not mean that you will not care. It does not mean that the insanity will lessen because you are choosing to live in a way that will give to you an uplift from the insanity. It does mean that you will be able to clearly change the way that you are living so that you can be free…free from the frequencies and programming that desires to direct your life, your thoughts, your decisions, your opinions, and your self-care. Now that seems to be quite a lot, doesn't it?

It is. There is quite a bit going on, my dears, and I do care so deeply for you and your journey toward awakening. And that is why I have asked to speak with you, to give to you a different way. I want to see you freed from the trappings of the insanity that seem to rule the earth. Are you ready? Would you like to hear a bit more? Perhaps you would like to try a little taste of what I am to give you.

I do understand any hesitancy on your part. After all, you have been what you call "sold a bill of goods" that has turned on you. Now everything isn't so bleak, of course not. But it seems that you have been struggling, even after you have awakened to truth. It seems that you have been disheartened, even after you have discovered a type of freedom in your beliefs. And it seems, my dears, that you have found yourself in what has been called a rut; that is, you are doing the same things, practicing the same spiritual ways and still you are not quite fulfilled.

Perhaps you feel that something, you don't know what, is missing? You have tried all of the ways to do your best. I have seen that. You have given and you have learned how to discern truth from untruth. Yet. Yes, there is that *yet*. I am here to tell you that one of the primary reasons that you seem to be still unfulfilled within your entire being is that there is a great occurrence upon the earth…and it is not going to go away any time soon.

You know, perhaps, of the battle upon the earth? The battle between truth and illusion, between wholeness of being and the illusion of separation from the whole? Yes, of course you know of this. You are awake. You are not really a beginner at all. And that is why I am speaking to you.

So then, why not give this a try? Why not dare to see what I am delivering to you, to assist you to remain separate from the insanity, separate from the illusion that says you must be a certain way in order to be spiritual, in order to be who you already are, and to assist you to more so, be free from the oppression so that you can truly stand and be who you are, discover the more of your own journey, and participate in the gallant journey of truth made manifest through incarnate awakened beings.

That is you. Ready?

-Teacher

I am Teacher and I am the same teacher who came forth long long ago, as I come forth now. I reach out to you, to uplift you, to assist the frequencies of that which you are, to dissolve the insanity, dissolve the illusion, and restore your conscious knowing; and in so doing, will there be restored the totality of all who have been breathed forth. Just as we have agreed…before the beginning of time.

-Teacher

SPEAKING ONE

*"This is not a way to deny what is occurring. It IS a way
to restore yourself, replenished in the grace of truth."*

Now let's just take a few deep breaths and bring yourself to that peaceful state that you so very much enjoy. Be sure that you are not having any other input, like the computer, the television or the phone or any other devise. Just you and I, Teacher.

What we will do together is discover that we are not the insanity not the confusion, not the horrific occurrences. But we are…the wholeness of being, the embracing of truth and more so, we are the light that shines evermore, even upon the insanity that we have uncovered and taken a good look at.

Yes, we have surely taken a good look at the insanity as it has been faithfully reported to us. That's all right that it is reported, of course. But I am here and you are here to reside in something else, that wonderful vibration called truth, wherein you and I and all beings can rest, replenish and go forth in a newly inspired way. So then, let's firstly do that. Let's reside in truth together. It's quite easy, you know.

All we need to do is remember, remember truth. Here's some of that which we can remember together. It's a feel-good kind of thing. Now when we enter this manner of being, we are not denying that horrors and the insanity that reside in physicality upon earth. We are participating in something together that sets those occurrences aside. It doesn't mean that you nor I don't care, of course we do. That is why we are troubled by what is occurring. So then you can let your mind rest in knowing that this is not a way to deny what is occurring. It IS a way to restore yourself, replenished in the grace of truth. How about that.

So then, let's just begin by speaking this truth. The one that says that you are not really a human being, but that your human nature is your vessel. Some of you are most aware of that truth. But what else is there to know about that? This.

The funny thing about illusion is that it seems to be so very real.

Though you have a very fine vessel, a human nature and a body-physical, they are vessels for the real you. And the real you is what I'd like to talk about with regard to truth. You see, the real you is waaay beyond the illusion. Now the funny thing about illusion is that it seems to be so very real. The illusion tells us that we are all separate beings and that we all have a path and that we all are...lost? Well, maybe not lost but not really found.

Let's just recognize two truths. The first is that you are a divine being, the One being, breathing yourself forth to be the many; the many who journey forth to what? To awaken and to continue awakening.

Now the second truth is that physicality is the adventure which holds the cause and effect of the awakening. Otherwise...what? Otherwise you would be who you really are and know it. You would be awake to the truth that you are one being, that all beings are one being and that there is nothing else that exists. Yet your mind can know that, but your consciousness wants to remember, to remember the reality of that truth. And that's why you are here.

So then, let's recognize that this physicality, though it is an illusion and resides within distortion, is an avenue within which we are residing...together.

Then the question might be, how can I reside within this journey which seems to be demonstrating horrific cause and effect, seems to be demonstrating insanity. How can I go forth? How can I go forth and not ignore the happenings, but still go forth in my best manner possible?

Ah! That is the real question and if you have asked that question, then I congratulate you. If you are just now thinking that is pretty good question, you are right where you need to be, right here and right now… with me.

When you receive these words, your mind will not know what to do with them.

I'd like to speak with you about some truths that might not fit within your mind, but I'll speak them anyway. Why? Because when you receive these words, your mind will not know what to do with them and it will have to wait. It will have to wait until the end of my speaking…and then it can try to figure out what it is that I am saying. And that is very fine indeed.

Long ago you entered this journey and began a process of forgetting and then remembering. It was a delightful process and you reveled in each awakening, each remembering of truth, truth that you were whole and not only embraced by love, but were love itself.

You found that to be most curious, curious that you forgot and then remembered and enjoyed the process. You wanted to understand what that was all about. And in your wanting, you called forth a teacher—a teacher who held the truth within the vibration of its being. The teacher spoke with you saying that you are remembering more. You didn't quite know what the teacher meant because you had forgotten the more.

And I am here now to remind you...again...of the more. Now there are many stories, ancient stories of those ones who came to earth, gods walking the earth who did not know that they were gods walking the earth. Yet when circumstances called forth certain abilities, the abilities were made manifest in these ones. The interesting or strange fact is that they never questioned why they had certain abilities when needed. They simply assumed that the abilities were part of who they were. And in truth, the abilities were part of who they were. Yet the more still remained forgotten.

And now here you are. You have certain abilities. You can know or have a feeling about what is about to happen, you have certain abilities that assist others to heal themselves, you are able to dip into the time stream and uncover the past and some of you can project yourself into the future and take a peek at what resides there. Some of you can allow other spirit beings to speak through you and some of you can simply know without words at all. And there are many more abilities.

Their mind couldn't reason that if they were the One, then how could they be the many?

Let me ask you something. Have you ever wondered why you have those abilities? You have perhaps reasoned that all beings have these abilities, but they simply haven't brought their consciousness to that expanded manner that would allow them to discover what it is that they are capable of. And you would be partly true in that the more that the gods of old did not recognize is that they were God…that God I Am, the One…and their mind couldn't reason that truth simply because if they were the One, then how could they be the many?

They knew that they were different than those who resided in sleep, those who suffered from the fears that ran rampant among the masses. And in those gods walking upon the earth, there was a compassion for those ones. And they entered the gatherings of the masses and spoke with them, some of them. Their words seemed to be a different language and the masses could not understand. The gods then retreated and wondered…wondered why the masses could not understand their words.

They decided to speak in a way that the masses would understand. That way was to incorporate some of the sleep state's beliefs, just a little, so that the masses could be uplifted a bit, be shown a different way. Then the gods returned to the people and loved them, spoke softly with them. The masses made them their leaders. It was not what was expected, yet in that position, the gods could help the masses more and more.

Little did the gods know that it was a trap. Not that anyone or anything deliberately set a trap. It was more that the distortion of physicality and their dipping into the sleep state led them to forget even more. They only knew that when they loved the people, the people became peaceful. The gods then continued in this manner...for eons.

You and the gods who walked the earth have both forgotten the same thing.

Now I would like to pause within this speaking of history and return to *you*. You and the gods who walked the earth have both forgotten the same thing. And your mind, the mind that rests within that human nature, will not know what to do with this. So just allow me to speak and you to receive.

Though many beliefs have been created about God, about Divinity, about what god is best; I know that you are beyond all of that and you know that to be true as well. Yet here is the fact. You are God I Am. Now that is not just a group of words. It is Truth. It is not *the* truth, not *a* truth. It is Truth itself, the vibration that forms as Truth.

You breathed yourself forth as the many and the many forgot. Then you breathed yourself forth as a few, a few who held the capability of remembering, of holding the vibration of Truth. Yet all who have been breathed forth are you. And, the you who is receiving these words are one of the many who can hold the vibration of Truth.

The you who is receiving these words are one of the many who can hold the vibration of Truth.

Now this doesn't make you special, more spiritual than the rest who cannot hold the vibration. Why? Well, my dear, because you are it. You are that Truth, whether you can remember or not. You are that called God I Am.

Now I know that many of you have heard or read those words. Yet I ask you: can you reside within that Truth? Can you reside within that frequency? Can you set aside the illusionary beingness of your personhood? Maybe. Maybe sometimes.

I am here to assist you to not only remember, but to continue to reside as the Truth of who you are: God I Am, or the One Being. And that is what we can be together, if you choose.

So then, I ask you to reflect upon what it is that you do not know, what it is that you hold within your belief system but have not yet experienced, and what the god walking the earth – you—did long ago and are just now remembering. Just reflect upon that, if you will, and I will speak with you again...not only speak with you, but reside with you in a way that will assist you to not only remember, but to be that which you are.

I am Teacher and I am the same teacher who came forth long long ago, as I come forth now. I reach out to you, to uplift you, to assist the frequencies of that which you are to dissolve the insanity, dissolve the illusion, and restore your conscious; knowing and in so doing, will there be restored the totality of all who have been breathed forth. Just as we have agreed... before the beginning of time.

While you are truly beyond the cause and effect, you have breathed it forth and reside within that which you breathed forth. You see, it is as if you have created within your imagination a story and then placed yourself within it. And the story has continued while you did dip yourself within it every once in a while. And now, now, my holy one, you are ready to be.

SPEAKING TWO

*All right now, we will continue. If you are first joining
me with this second speaking, I ask that you return
to the very beginning. Why? The words and the
arrangement of the words hold a vibrational frequency
and that frequency is a match to the truth that resides
within your consciousness, waiting to be made known.
You cannot hurry this process, this journey that we are
taking together. In truth, there is no such thing as hurry,
as we are stepping outside the boundaries of time itself.*

Then I will continue. Once again take a few
deep breaths and relax a bit, setting aside the
cause and effect beyond this moment. Just bring
yourself to right here and right now.

Now I am speaking to you, the god who is incarnate and who has forgotten the truth of who you
are. It isn't right or wrong that you have forgotten,
more so, it is something that you have been enjoying
for quite some time, many many lifetimes. Until now.
Now you are residing within the deep forgetting. You
have the concept of this truth, yet the reality evades

you. And that is why we are together now, right now.

Long ago we did agree upon this moment, this moment when I would come forth to assist you to remember…everything. This is the first part of that remembering. And you might be wondering why the entire remembering cannot occur right now. And the answer is this.

You will be adjusting to the vibrational frequencies of truth. You, the real you, do not need to adjust to anything. You are everything, after all. Yet you are incarnate and wish to remain incarnate. Then in order to allow your physicality, your vessel, to remain incarnate, there is a gradual receiving and integrating of these frequencies, the vibration of Truth itself. And what is Truth itself, but you, the Totality of You.

You are not lost, even though you might have felt lost within the cause and effect that is currently occurring upon earth. You have resided at this moment many times. What is this moment? It is the battle, the battle to be. What or who is battling? Truth and Illusion. You see, that called illusion—and distorting that resides therein—has developed a type of consciousness and within it, a manner of holding the masses within it, harvesting the energies of those who strive to be more, not knowing that they are the more itself; the sleeping masses. The sleeping masses are those that you breathed forth long ago, breathing yourself forth to reside, to journey, to experience awakening incarnate.

Then now, again, is the battle, as it has raged itself over and over again, sometimes retreating as if it has been completed, only to rise again to discover victory. And you are here, not to enter into the battle, as you have many times in the past of these histories.

You are now here to remember, remember fully within the entirety of your being. You have not yet experienced this moment in all of your previous journeys within physicality. You have thrilled within those journeys, yet you returned to One before you could actually know that One while incarnate.

Because this battle has raged on and on, the opportunity to know while incarnate presents itself as part of the balancing within the cause and effect. And while you are truly beyond the cause and effect, you have breathed it forth and reside within that which you breathed forth.

You see, it is as if you have created within your imagination a story and then placed yourself within it. And the story has continued while you did dip yourself within it every once in a while. And now, now, my holy one, you are ready to be.

Now all of this might seem to be a bit illusive;

yet even hearing or receiving these words begins the shifting of your frequencies and this shifting, then, begins your detaching from the histories, from the need to be asleep in order to experience awakening, and begins your detaching from hiding yourself from yourself. When I say *begins*, I mean that you are now integrating the frequencies of which I have spoken.

Do not allow your human nature, your vessel, to fear what is occurring or what will occur. This is all part of your journey, the journey that would one day lead you to know the Truth of who you are, while incarnate. That is this journey, I am most pleased to report to you.

Truth can dispel all illusion and distortion.

Now breathe deeply and allow this beginning integrating to occur. You will, of course, continue to be able to reside within your journey each day; yet know this to be true: You will perhaps begin to experience a type of detaching from the emotional cause and effect. This does not mean that you do not care about what is occurring upon your earth. Not at all.

It does mean that you are beginning to reside in a manner that will allow you to go forth as you intend to go forth, and more so, to affect the yearning of the masses to be uplifted from the insanity that prevails. In a manner of speaking, you might say that you are beginning to make a difference and that difference resides in Truth. Truth can dispel all illusion and distortion. That is you. Truth.

And as you have breathed yourself forth as the many who are now receiving these words, then it is natural to know that you, as these many, have a great capability to reach into the illusion and unite with that of yourself, that which is asleep and wanting the awakening, the relief, the restoration to occur.

Breathe deeply and allow Truth to reside. You are more residing as Truth than you have ever done before. Allow. You cannot make anything happen. That would be your human nature trying to figure out how to cause this process to become more real. Yet it is not as real to your human nature as it is within the Truth of Your very own Being.

I will speak again with you.

I, Teacher, am here to take you by the hand and guide you safely through the obstacles of the cause and effect so that you can step upon firm ground, upon the known, as you go forth.

SPEAKING THREE

*The foundation of the better way begins with the truth
that all beings are one being, that the divine essence
doesn't come by the pound.*

*Oh I am most pleased that you have decided to continue
in this process of living in a way that can set aside the
external world, where does the insanity reside, and live
within your fulfillment, as you continue to remember
who you really are.*

Now you might become a bit tired of hearing
the words—remembering who you really
are—yet I can assure you that once you do
remember—really remember and know deep inside
of your being—then you will not be presented with
those words at all. They will have fulfilled their
purposes.

Now as we continue in this journey together I,
Teacher, am here to take you by the hand and guide
you safely through the obstacles of the cause and effect so that you can step upon firm ground, upon the

known, as you go forth. So then, the first ingredient is trust. I am asking you to trust that what I am leading you toward is real and is not only safe, but more so, is a way of living that will bring you more than a moment of inner peace.

While you are experiencing inner peace, the external world cannot touch you.

Now the reason that inner peace is so very important is that while you are experiencing inner peace, the external world cannot touch you. That is to say, you can reside within inner peace and walk among the masses, some of whom are in deep sleep, and not be pulled into the vibrations of desperation, and the rest of survival's grasp.

Now you might think that you can do this already, yet at times you experience your own battle with fears, fear of not having enough money, fear of getting old and incapacitated, fear of losing the ones you love, fear of not being able to make your house or rent payment…many fears. All fears of losing what you have. Now if you are living in the cause and effect and are asleep to truth, it is most natural to have those fears. It is most natural that those fears rule your life, your thinking and your actions.

Fears are resting upon an illusion that is so debilitating that one can hardly believe it.

So then I am taking your hand and beginning this journey by telling you that fears are resting upon an illusion that is so debilitating that one can hardly believe it. Now you have heard this before, yet stay with me because I am going to connect the dots. The illusion, you will remember, tells you that you are a separate being from all the others. It tells you simply because residing in the physical demonstrates this illusion because everyone is living inside a separate body.

And this illusion is at the foundation of all fears. It tells you that you are alone, even if you don't say the words, even if you are surrounded by family and friends.

The illusion or the foundation of all fear says that you and all beings are lost...and there doesn't seem to be a way to be found. Yes, there are certain religions that embrace their people, yet even they say that the ones who are not with them are not going to make it. And yes, there are some gatherings of beings, some religious or spiritual gatherings, that have dedicated themselves to embracing all who come.

Yet here we go again. It is not the fault of any religion or gathering that beneath all good intentions, there is the "them and us" scenario. Now I am not saying that so that you can defend a religion or gathering. More so, I am taking your hand and asking you to follow along just a few steps at a time toward a better way.

Divine essence doesn't come by the pound.

The foundation of the better way begins with the truth that all beings are one being, that the divine essence doesn't come by the pound. That is, divinity isn't separated to a little here for this being and a little there for that being, and if you hold your mouth right or say the right words, you get a little more divinity than the others. It just doesn't work that way. And the reason that it doesn't work that way is because you and all beings are divinity itself. The whole.

Now here is where we get a little light on words and heavy on the vibration of the truth that we are sharing. It is time to remember, time to at least accept the fact that the divine spark of creation flows forth and resides within that body; that divine spark is also called the life force. What do you think that is?

The life force that resides in everything? What do you think that really is? You might have some thoughts on the answer, you might not.

The life force is the spark of creation flowing forth

from the wholeness, the All, that called God I Am. And it flows forth and resides within that vessel, your body, your human, your persona. Yet that life force is who you are. Get it? That is the real you.

The life force inside that body is you. That is who you are.

And the real you is the same real you that resides in every body, in every human, in every human's projected persona. Now do you see? Take a moment to let that sink in. I know some of you have heard the words before; but let the reality sink in. The life force inside that body is you. That is who you are.

And in order to be incarnate, you must reside within a human nature, within a body-physical and within some kind of persona, which allows you to journey through the cause and effect. That, my dears, is what is going on…and you are asking of yourself to wake up to that fact.

And when you refuse to accept that fact and choose to remain asleep because the truth can't fit into your belief systems, you are also choosing to live within the fear and to deliver your energies, your hopes and dreams, to that fear as it feeds the illusion and those who rule the illusion. Now that is just plain nasty, isn't it? Then that is why we are together

...so that you can choose differently.

Then why not, for this moment, choose differently. Why not say to yourself, all right, I am going to give this a try. I am going to believe that the real identity of me is the life force. That is what I am. And the rest are simply vehicles within which I can live so that I can be incarnate, so that I can journey, so that I can experience the amazing purpose-fulfilled of continued awakening.

Within remembering truth is the shifting of your entire system.

Within continued awakening, oh things get jumbled around a little in the beginning. That's because you are adjusting your frequencies, and physicality is adjusting to a new you, one who is remembering truth. Within remembering truth is the shifting of your entire system.

After a while, physicality and the cause and effect begin to be nice to you; that is, things begin to even out and you also begin to notice the little serendipitous things that cause you to smile.

After a while, those happenings cause you to dare to think that you might be taken care of, that there is something bigger occurring in your life and you are not sure that you can trust it, but you are going to keep on doing what you are doing. And that is, you are remembering who you really are, even as you go forth in your day giving the illusion that you are your human vessel.

Now I'd like to give you another little tidbit, one that will help you to be free, free from the horrors that tend to pull you and everyone in, simply because you are astounded by what is happening. The tidbit is this.

Before you enter into anything that will deliver to you news of what seems to be occurring upon the earth, before you read the news or watch it on your screen, I ask you to speak these words to yourself. Just take a deep breath and bring yourself to a peaceful state.

Then whisper these words to yourself: *I am the spark of creation taking form in the physical. All beings are the same as am I. We are all here to remember this truth, to awaken to the full knowing that there is nothing that we need do to become holy. We are the holiness itself.*

Then go forth in your day. You might find that you are not so very interested in the news as you previously were. Oh you are not the ostrich with your head in the sand; you are an awakening being who chooses, chooses to live in a manner that gives to you a better way.

You are an awakening being who chooses, chooses to live in a manner that gives to you a better way.

Next, remember that the cause and effect is giving you the option to believe that you are here to suffer and that there is a magic way to end suffering. Then you will be given certain things to do, money to pay, gatherings to belong to, and eventually, if you continue, you will begin to get ready to move to the next level of getting closer to God.

But the truth is, you are that God that they are holding above you like a carrot, saying that if you make yourself holy, you can have a taste. Don't you think that is so wrong? It is. It is all part of the sleep state. And many believe it. You cannot make them wake up and see the wrongness, see the truth instead. Just as you were not ready long ago, then now they are not quite ready.

Then as you go forth, refuse. Refuse to rest in fear and instead rest in the knowing of your true identity. Now being the creative life force, being God I Am incarnate doesn't mean that you will be able to move mountains, make the banks to drop their millions in into your lap, or more realistically, make the world stop its insanity. Remembering who you are is more subtle, yet more powerful in a different way.

And this is why you want to continue to experience this truth. Experience. That is different from intellectual knowing. The more that you go forth, holding this truth within your Self, the more that you will be living in the vibrations that flow forth from that truth. Now this might seem to be inconsequential, might seem to be not a very good reason to continue. Yet hear my words.

You are not going forth to the sea and holding up your arms and making the sea part itself, so that you can walk through. This is bigger.

The more that you go forth in your day within this remembering, the more physicality will part itself for you. What does that mean? You are not going forth to the sea and holding up your arms and making the sea part itself, so that you can walk through. This is bigger.

You are going forth in your day, remembering that the real you is Divine, is the Life Force residing incarnate; and when you go forth in this manner, the illusion pulls away from you. What does that mean?

It means that the difficulties caused by the untruth and the fears and anxieties, begin to diminish. It's as if there is a solution to everything, though you might not know how the solutions will come about, you simply know…you know that you are living in a different way, you know that you are observing the illusion differently. You are recognizing that everything that pushes people away from each other—making some special and some not—all of those ways are part of the untruth saying that you and the others are not the same. But you are. You are the same Divine Essence. You are the same life force.

And here it is: you are not separate from each other. You breathe the same breath. Your heart beats the same pulsating beat. Your mind gathers truth and tries to bend it to your own knowing. Your inner knowing realizes that you are all one being, one organism if you will. And the final tidbit that you realize is that all of this is just wonderful.

This beginning is the real foundation of what we will do together.

Now this beginning of this journey that I am inviting you to enter is the real foundation of what we will do together. Why not go back to the beginning of this third speaking and receive it again. The more that you receive these words, words that we created together long ago, words that are designed to change your vibrational frequencies…the frequencies that the life force journeys forth within…and when that change occurs, you are more who you really are and less of who you have believed yourself to be.

Put another way, you are less of the survival and its horrific cause and effect, and you are more of truth and its light-filled way of living where everything seems to fall into place so much so that it actually puts a little smile upon your face and that smile seems to want to stay put. Yes, that feeling. It says that this is real and there is much more to come.

You perhaps saw that little statement that said that you and I created these words together. So…they might not be that strange, eh?

Even the creatures, that of nature, the earth...all of everything is comprised by the same life force. And the reason that you want to remember this truth is so that you can go forth as the whole, so that you can go forth knowing that there is nothing created that is going to go against you.

SPEAKING FOUR

With these words, you are waking up to truth and how it is made manifest as your journey.

Now the next part of this journey that we created together requires the understanding of reality, the real thing and not that which is projected forth as an interpretation of the cause and effect and its past missteps and near-fulfillments.

In order to understand reality, let's take a look at what it is not. Reality is not a struggle. Well, let's admit that within the sleep state, struggle is the primary ingredient. Yet you are removing yourself from the sleep state. Even with these words, you are waking up more and more, waking up to truth and how it is made manifest *as* your journey.

The real manner of residing in physicality requires that you, once again, remember that everything is all made out of the same life force. That is, even the creatures, that of nature, the earth...all of everything is comprised by the same life force. And the reason that you want to remember this truth is so that you can forth as the whole, so that you can go forth knowing that there is nothing created that is going to go against you.

Now here is one truth: anything that is created without the life force will not remain. What does that mean? There are those who create for the purpose of making money. Now that isn't a wrong action; yet there is a missing ingredient. When there is any kind of creation, if the person reaches within him- or herself before participating with the force of creation, if the person reaches within him- or herself and unites consciously with that which is called the divine essence which flows forth from the core of your being; it is then real creation! Yes, then there is a real creation occurring—whether it is for money or not.

Now there is nothing wrong with money. I'm not saying that at all. What I am saying is that there is a greater purpose for creating. If the creation is for beauty and there is a monetary exchange, that is different. Why? Simply because a creation of real beauty flows forth from the core of creation and the divine life force forms itself, partnering with your physicality to create something beautiful. Do you see?

We are speaking of the much bigger picture, the journey within which you are able to remain true to who you really are.

Now you could be thinking that there are many wonderful things created and they seem to be lasting. Yes, they seem to be. Yet in the bigger picture, they hold no presence, none at all. And we are speaking of the much bigger picture, the journey within which you are able to remain true to who you really are and the journey within which you will go forth and experience all expressions as a recognizing of truth and its support of your very presence. Now that might sound a bit far-fetched, but it is not. This is exactly what we have created together.

And we created in this manner...because why? Because we saw what could be called *the projected future*. We saw what would occur if the sleep state continued in its density, becoming more and more residing upon fear and the loss of self. We saw this, and we firstly decided to create this way of being so that you—all of you who receive this—could be uplifted from survival's grasp.

And then we created this way of being so that while you are journeying forth within the reality of truth, your divine manner of being would flow forth and affect the whole, be as a beacon to those who are wanting some relief from the struggle, be a shining light for those who have given up all hope. First your removal from survival's grasp in all forms; and then you would automatically be that beacon of light, of truth, of divine essence journeying forth for the pleasure of the journey.

This is the beginning of your freedom.

Now the reality of which I have been speaking is nothing new, yet it might be new to your belief system. The best way to be open to what I am about to deliver to you is to set your beliefs aside. You can easily do this simply by deciding that you will firstly receive what we have created together and then later you can try to understand it through your own beliefs. Yet be forewarned. Your beliefs will change, will transform, will release any hold from developing upon the foundation of fear itself. Yes, this is the beginning of your freedom.

So then I am going to speak our words to you and you are going to receive them, just as we planned long ago. This part of this journey together is called *receiving*. It's easy because you are not asking of yourself to do anything but receive our words. You aren't even deciding if you believe them, if they are real or if they can benefit you. You are just receiving.

So then take a deep breath, relax a little and receive the words we created long ago:

I am much more than I have been led to believe. Through no one's fault have I been led to believe that I am merely a human who struggles through life itself. I have awakened to the truth that I am the life force itself. I hold within the core of by being, the divine spark of creation. All of this is all that I am. Any other concept is but an untruth which was created upon the illusion, upon the untruth of separation from the whole. There is not separation. There is only the whole.

All studies, all readings, all venturing forth in search of truth have benefited me greatly. Even if the studies were distorted a bit, still they assisted me to journey toward my own awakening. And now I am awake. I am no longer in need of the fears that held me captive in survival. I am no longer in need of the beliefs that say that anyone is better than another. I am the whole and the whole is that which I am.

All questionings have benefited me in that they have developed my ability to discern, to discern the nature of truth and the nature of the illusion. The untruths of survival will not touch me because I am awake to them and my own being recoils from them.

Joy and delight, laughter and deep sighs are all part of my new manner of being, my new manner of going forth into the cause and effect. My light flows forth and darkness removes itself from the place where my steppings reside.

I am all beings and all beings are that which I am. Yet there are also many who are residing in truth, as am I. And we do go forth in celebration of truth and in our celebration, there begins a rippling of light, of divine essence, flowing forth from us into the distortion.

As our divine light flows forth into the distortion, those who are reaching out for hope, for some kind of relief from the suffering, from the insanity; those ones feel the presence of truth and weep for the knowing that they are not alone. This is the beginning of incarnating the truth, the reality that all are one.

Each being who is trapped in survival's grasp is simply residing in the unknown to themselves. The unknown that the survival is an illusion, that there is truth in every breath. Yet this tiny awakening requires that they let go of holding on to anything that resides created from fear, as all fear rests as the foundation of survival and the illusion and distortion.

When there is a glimmer of hope, where there is a glimmer of your radiating light, there is a breath, a divine breath that flows forth to kiss the hearts of those who can no longer bear the insanity.

And as you go forth, you are simply knowing that this flowing forth is automatic from your being, is automatically reaching out in union with the totality of that which you are. Do you see? You will have removed yourself from insanity's grasp, you will have begun to go forth knowing truth and being truth itself. And as you go forth, the fulfillment of our purposes created long ago will be fulfilled.

You see, you are yourself and you are also those ones who are asleep. Divine Essence flowing forth as the many. You are the many. You are the All. Now don't let those words bring your mind and your beliefs up front before we are finished with this part of our journey together. Just sit back and firstly receive. Then I will continue.

Truth and the reality of truth hold within them a vibrational frequency and that frequency is a direct match with the encodings that reside within the fabric of your being.

Now all that I have been saying is much more

than words. Truth and the reality of truth hold within them a vibrational frequency and that frequency is a direct match with the encodings that reside within the fabric of your being. You placed those encodings therein for the specific purpose of activating automatically when your consciousness expanded and was able to hold truth, the reality of truth. This is that time. This is that moment.

Truth does not fit into belief systems. Yet certain belief systems can lead a being toward truth. You see, there comes a moment when there is a realization that Truth is not able to be spoken, that words limit the immensity of Truth itself. Yet there is still Truth and the residing within the full knowing of truth.

Remember, knowing and understanding are different from each other. Knowing is your inner knowing of truth itself. Yet it does flow forth to enter the portal of your vessels—your human nature, your body-physical, and the persona through which your human journeys. When the known flows forth and enters those vessels, there is a shift in the frequencies of the manifesting of your incarnate self. That is to say, the entirety of your being changes.

There is a type of distortion that occurs when the mind fits the known into a belief system.

And the mind wants to understand everything; that is its nature. And through its efforting to understand, it tries to fit the known, the truth, into some kind of belief system. Now this isn't a crime, yet there is a type of distortion that occurs when the mind fits the known into a belief system.

This means that when you seem to understand truth, you would do well to remember that there will always be a missing ingredient in such understanding simply because truth, the reality of truth, is not made manifest through belief systems. You could say, then, that truth itself remains a bit of a mystery to the mind, to understanding.

Now all of this does in no way mean that you cannot or do not reside in the full knowing of that which you are. That is what this is all about. You are now, even in this moment, beginning to let go of an attachment to your previous journey, previous to beginning to receive the words that we created together long ago. And in letting go of an attachment to who you believe you have developed yourself to be, there is a kind of peace that enters your consciousness. It is the peace that says that you can stop trying so hard to be that which you already are: divinity incarnate.

This first stepping is of major significance to your fulfillment of being.

In letting go of the attachment to your previous journey, in letting go of who you have believed you are and have become; there is the first stepping upon the new path, upon a new way of residing incarnate. This first stepping is of major significance to your fulfillment of being, to your being able to go forth amidst the darkness and to never fear nor shrink from your own journey.

This first stepping is your celebration of daring to be who you really are, of daring to go forth in a way that is unfamiliar yet so very comforting that you cannot depart from your new way. This first stepping holds you within it and embraces you with love, with peace, with joy, with what is called safety; yet there is no concern for safety simply because the darkness abhors the light that you are.

Now I ask you to take a deep breath, to sigh a little, and to rest. I also ask you to allow these words to simply be and to wait at least one entire day before you receive them again. The vibrational frequencies are working within your system now, pushing aside the untruth and lighting the way for the flowing forth of the known into your consciousness.

Now the flowing forth of the known into your consciousness is not the same as studying the words and trying to figure out what they mean and how they apply to you. That would be your mind's action, which is all right. Yet there is something magnificent that occurs first and it is that the divine known, truth itself, flows forth into your consciousness. Conscious knowing. Truth incarnate. You knowing who you are.

Yes, that's the real thing. Then just take a few breaths and if you can, go out into nature even for just a few moments. There, in nature, can you discover the match to those frequencies that are flowing forth, dancing their way through the untruth, dispersing those patterns that are residue of past fears, and creating that pathway for the real you to be known by the real you.

Then until we speak again, isn't it just wonderful knowing that you are not alone, that you cannot possibly be, and that the wholeness is beauty itself, and requires nothing from you simply because it is all that you are. You to you. Yes!

You are not here to be overcome by the distortion, by the insanity, and by its manifestation in the lives of the masses who are asleep and are victims to that distortion and insanity. You are not here to allow yourself to be a victim within your compassion for others. You are here for something else.

SPEAKING FIVE

We are together entering into something powerfully magnificent.

Now let's enter into the next phase of what we are proceeding to experience together, shall we? The next phase asks you to take an action. It's this.

This phase, which we are entering into right at this moment as we speak together, asks you to reflect upon something, just a little something. It asks you to search your inner being for the fears that seem to hide themselves within the name of *concerns*. Now there is nothing wrong with concerns or fears for that matter. Yet we are together entering into something powerfully magnificent.

Then just take a moment, right now, to ask yourself: what am I concerned about? Begin with yourself. Later we can ask the same about others in your life and further of earth and all that is occurring. But for now, let's begin with you. What concerns do you hold within your being?

Now a hint might be, are you concerned about health, about weight, about aging, about money, about marrying or not, about having children or not, about a partner or not? Are you concerned that your work isn't fulfilling and you believe that it should be? Are you concerned that your spiritual journey is not as much as it should be or that you want it to be? What are your concerns?

Now if you would take a paper and pen, or your computer, and just write a list of your concerns. No need to be cautious about what you write because the information is only for you, for your eyes. I'll wait until you do that.

Good. Now if you haven't done that yet, then please do so. The remainder of this speaking will not benefit you one bit if you don't participate. It would be like trying to decide if you like a certain drink without even tasting it.

Now with this list of concerns, I'd like you to think of them as fears, even if they are mini fears. Just look at each one and ask yourself, what is the projected possible future that the mini fear rests upon?

For example, if you are concerned—or have a mini fear—about health, perhaps your projected mini fear is that you will not be able to either continue with good health, regain good health, or will experience disease or disabilities. Now just reading those words won't do much. Your really have to look inside and find that fear. What form does it take?

The hidden fears are the weight that holds us all down, especially when we are nearing that divine joy and delight

You see, the hidden fears are the weight that holds us all down, especially when we are nearing that divine joy and delight, that divine blissful state that says that "I am"...period. Just "I am". So then you can see that uncovering those concerns and fears is most helpful in clearing the way for your residing in a new frequency, leaving the insanity behind.

Now I'd like to speak a little about that *leaving the insanity behind*. I'm not saying that you are living in the insanity or that you are insane. More so, I am saying that we created this together so that you would not be pulled into the insanity that is occurring in the sleep state upon earth. And the ways that one could be pulled into that insanity are many but also easy to recognize.

You can recognize when you are being pulled into the insanity of the cause and effect upon earth by observing your emotions. If you hear or read the news and what has just occurred is so horrific to you that you can hardly believe it is occurring...again; and you feel as if you must hold yourself so that you won't crumble, or you feel that you must weep because the horrific events are overwhelming...if you feel any of this, you are a loving, caring, being, of course. Yet.

Yet, you are not here to be overcome by the distortion, by the insanity, and by its manifestation in the lives of the masses who are asleep and are victims to that distortion and insanity. You are not here to allow yourself to be a victim within your compassion for others. You are here for something else.

You are here to remove yourself vibrationally from the insanity, from the frequencies that reside within the hate and viciousness of the insanity. You are here to reside in the light of who you really are and once established within the essence of truth, you are here to breathe forth that truth, that light, that divine wholeness of being.

And you can do this simply by remembering who you are and by taking the time to establish your union with truth. Then. Then you can go forth. Does this mean that if you hear of something occurring that is horrible beyond horrible that you will have no feelings whatsoever? Of course not. You are residing within a human vessel.

Not one being is separate from the whole. We have already established that, yet it doesn't hurt to be reminded…often.

Yet you are divine and within your divinity you will easily be able to remember that you are not one being, but that you are all beings and all beings are the one being. This means that you will be able to refuse to attach your being to the distortion and the horrors, and instead be able to breathe forth truth for those who are suffering, for those who are trapped in the sleep and distortion, trapped in the illusion that they are alone and separate from their own divine self…which of course is impossible. Not one being is separate from the whole. We have already established that, yet it doesn't hurt to be reminded…often.

So then, back to your concerns or fears. Write what the real fear is and then, my dears, recognize that they are all resting upon illusion, the illusion says that this might or might not happen, but all that is…nothing. Absolutely nothing. Just make believe. It has been a way that has led you to believe that you can protect yourself from harm, from the seeming inevitable, by keeping a fear-based concern alive. Of course, even as I say the words, you can see how futile and useless such a manner is. And more so, how debilitating those fears are. Remember, they are resting upon nothing.

Yet before you read those words and just agree with them, I do ask you to look at each one that you have written and recognize the untruth that does not exist. If you are residing in this moment, right here and right now, then all of those concerns are make believe. Take a moment to recognize this. Remember, this action is one that will free you from attachments to the insanity.

Now I am going to speak some words again, to you. They are different, of course, yet they will hold the same purpose as previously. The purpose is to assist your frequencies to vibrate in such a manner that your consciousness will expand and you will be assisted to enter into a more inclusive you, the you who you have always been. Each and every part of our speaking together is devoted to exactly that.

Then these are the words that we have created long ago to fulfill this purpose.

In the beginning of time there resided those beings who entered the frequencies of physicality, physicality that was not yet dense but was as if pre-dense. And as those beings entered the forming of physicality, they too began to form.

It wasn't that they were without form, yet when they entered the newly forming physicality, their presence brought to the forming of physicality, a call. The call was one that invited physicality to support and hold within it those who had entered. It was as if physicality became a substance that held the beings within it, and even though there was not a question or even an answer, the forming then held that purpose.

The beings, of course, had no knowing of the forming of the purpose of physicality, that it would hold them within it and further, care for them. The beings were new to physicality itself.

As they then did journey within their exploration of the whole as it was being made manifest as the many, they discovered several frequencies that formed themselves before them. The frequencies continued to pulsate into physicality until there did form a creature, first one and then another and then another. And physicality itself did them embrace those creatures and did hold them within it and care for them.

The creations within physicality were many and the beings and the creatures resided as companions, enjoying the discovery of movement and the presence of physicality forming itself as if just for them. In truth, physicality was forming itself "just for them".

And now I am here to tell you that that pattern and purpose has never changed. Physicality was formed for the purpose of supporting and holding within it the caring of those beings who also took form. Even though such caring and holding is barely recognizable now, still it remains.

And it is within this purpose and truth that you will be able to go forth, once again, and recognize the truth of that which was, is, and will be…until the entirety of all releases its journey and resides as One once again. Yet do not allow those words to fool you. Always is everything one, yet the flowing forth into physicality has given the illusion of separation from that Oneness by the very nature of physicality. We *seem* to be individual beings.

And you have journeyed here to deliver to yourself the great pleasure that you once, long long ago, experienced in your first steppings upon earth in the physicality that formed here, holding you within it. You are here to experience the gift and to reside within it, as you go forth leaving the insanity behind and radiating light, truth, and fulfillment of One to all…to all.

Now I believe you have received sufficient vibrational frequencies to assist you to rest for a while, un-til we meet again. Yet do not continue to receive my next speaking until you have waited at least one full day.

Then we will now simply enjoy the truth that has flowed forth for your knowing.

When you view something, anything, and you place an interpretation upon it, you have then successfully ceased its movement and created it to be as your beliefs and then interpretations would have it to be.

SPEAKING SIX

*During this speaking, we will enter into those
frequencies that will dissolve the illusion.*

*Now in this speaking, we will begin to be more and more
divine and less and less residing in the illusion that we
must do something to become divine, to become more of
who we already are.*

Y ou have perhaps heard those words before, but
this is different. It is not only hearing the words.
More so, during this speaking, we will enter
into those frequencies that will dissolve the illusion.
What does that mean?

Remember the fears and concerns? And do you
remember that they were all resting upon nothing?
Upon something negative projected into the future
so that...why? Why were you participating in your
journey in that manner?

Survival demands that each being project a possible difficulty, grave or small, into the future so that he
or she can be ready, can prepare for whatever might

occur, so that they won't be a victim to the struggle again. Yet. Yet projecting into the future the possible forming of the fears is just that. It is making each being a victim of something that has not yet occurred and perhaps will never occur.

In this manner, you are experiencing ahead of time, suffering. Survival has trained everyone well. It has invited you—everyone—to suffer, even when there might not be a reason to suffer. Survival says that if you project into the future a possible difficulty—grave or small—that you will then have a reason to suffer—ahead of time.

Now that is curious, isn't it? *Ahead of time* means that you have stepped beyond the current moment and journeyed into the possible future and placed there a good reason to suffer; and then, you have returned to the present and begun to suffer, to react, to have a fear or concern about that projection. And as we have recognized together, none of this is real. Nothing.

Yet you have practiced this manner of being over and over again. And I would like to talk about what you have come to be very good at, and that is that you have been able to project yourself into the possible future. That means that you are most adept at traveling the time stream. And now we want to become more conscious of that ability, leaning how we can participate with the time stream in a positive, more beneficial manner. Yes!

So then now you have begun to let go of projecting negativity and possible difficulties into the future simply because you have no need or use for suffering an illusionary manifestation that continues to speak the untruth that you are separate from the whole and must struggle "all by yourself". We are clear on that, aren't we? Of course! Yet you might want to reflect upon that little statement so that you can be fully awake to the past patterns and also be clear of your choice to refuse to participate in that manner...ever again.

Oh you might find yourself feeling the old concern creep up, but its vibration is deadening, heavy and causing the delight and joy of freedom to screech to a halt. You will feel it and then in that moment, will you be able to say to yourself, *"No, I'm not thinking that way any longer. It is not for me."* Or words of your own choosing. And that is exactly what you are doing. You are awake and you are choosing, choosing how you will experience the present moment, the here and now. And holding fear or concern or heaviness about something that doesn't exist, is nothing, is the easy choice: no.

So then let's talk about the time stream and how you are naturally able to project into the possible future. Firstly I would like to speak with you about objective viewing. You see, when you view something, anything, and you place an interpretation upon it, you have then successfully ceased its movement and created it to be as your beliefs and then interpretations would have it to be.

Now proceeding in this manner is quite detrimental to recognizing truth. Why? Let's use this example. If you are having a vision, if you are thinking about something and the thought gives to you a scenario, you then find the next action that you take is to interpret that vision or that scenario. I'm not talking so much about is this right or wrong, but more so, the interpretation itself.

When you interpret instead of allowing, you are actually refusing the presence of what is.

When you interpret instead of allowing, you are actually refusing the presence of what is. And I am speaking about this for the primary reason that we are going to view the possible future and while viewing, I will be asking you to remain objective and simply view.

For example, if we are viewing the possible future and you see something that might have a meaning and a conclusion to you, then you are not objective-ly viewing. If you see two people walking and they are communicating in whispers, you will be tempted to interpret the reason for their whispering. Yet in that moment, you really do not know why they are whispering. You only view, objectively, that they are whispering.

It is a habit that invites us all to interpret. Why? We are accustomed to placing our human nature, our persona, into that viewing and then we become part of it, influencing the frequencies without even being aware that we are influencing. In our projected view-ing into the future, we are most definitely wanting to remain objective for two reasons.

Firstly, we want to be able to receive the vision, the information without changing its nature and its presentation. And secondly, we are dedicated to not interpreting with that vision. And then a third rea-son is that we do not want to take to ourselves an attachment, to place ourselves into the future and flow our frequencies there; this habit, as we have dis-covered by examining our fears and concerns, does us no good but inhibits our ability to remain in this moment, right here and right now.

Then let us speak a little about the time stream and its presentations of the possible future. How can there be a possible future? The time stream holds for us the illusion of cause and effect in a way that tells us or leads us to believe that there is a real journey. And I suppose we could admit that there is a journey, yet it resides in the moment. If a journey resides in the moment, then there is only now. Yet there is the time stream and the seeming journey within which we are residing. How can all of this be?

The answer resides in the reason for the time stream, the reason for the journey, the reason for the cause and effect. And all of those reasons have to do with you and who you are and why you are incarnate. Yes, it might be true that you have placed before yourself a purpose, a desire to accomplish something. And that is neither good nor bad, true or untrue. It simply is something that you have decided, determined.

And within that determining or not determining, there resides truth. The truth is that you entered this journey, this moment within the time stream, to hold truth, to reach into the density of the illusion and place therein truth, light and fulfillment of consciously knowing of One, consciously knowing that all are one and that all are created within divine essence.

Now as you can tell by those words, you are not going to take an action that will breathe itself into that density...without firstly knowing what you are doing beyond the desire to do what you came here to do. And knowing what you are doing begins with understanding the time stream and your participation with it.

Now just take a deep breath and relax for a moment so that the changing frequencies can catch up with themselves, so to speak. You have been receiving words that you didn't expect to receive and you are waiting now to hear about the time stream and how you can participate with it, even though the only thing that really exists is right here and right now. This means that your mind is going to be very present so that it can figure that out, so that it can make sense of what we are speaking about.

This is about change and further, it is all about stepping into your new manner of being, of residing in truth and about leaving the insanity behind.

So then when you take that deep breath and relax for a moment, you are also letting go of the desire or seeming need to place everything in a row so that your intellectuality can feel comfortable. This is not about feeling comfortable. This is about change and further, it is all about stepping into your new manner of being, of residing in truth and about leaving the insanity behind.

Firstly, let's speak about why we would be viewing, objectively, the possible future. Well, the answer resides in the past, the seeming past, where you and I determined that we would participate in this present moment, in the physicality that has been created for the purpose of experiencing awakening to truth. And as I have spoken, we discovered that there was a possible battle, a battle between the sleep state and truth. It sounds like an easy win, doesn't it? Yet there we perceived a battle where the darkness of untruth held the multitudes in suffering, in the insanity of horrors upon horrors.

And as we viewed, it was then that you and I decided that we would reside here, right here and right now, and we would participate with truth. Now participating with truth is an impossibility actually, simply because truth is. So then it means that we decided to reside in truth and in so doing, we would be participating in the fulfillment of purpose, the incarnating within physicality of consciously knowing truth. Consciously.

Even though the time stream portends to be a flowing forth of events, the truth remains that all time is in the moment.

So then we had viewed the time stream and made a decision based upon what was the possible future. Yet. You see here we reside within another truth, one that will ask you to expand your consciousness and perhaps allow your beliefs to shift and change. Even though the time stream portends to be a flowing forth of events, the truth remains that all time is in the moment. Then what has occurred to give the impression to all who reside incarnate, that there is a journey, a flowing forth, a residing in what seems to be the past, the present and then what will be the future?

It is this. In the early residing within physicality and with our creatures and being held within and being cared for by physicality forming itself, we learned how to stretch time. We learned how to expand the present moment and in so doing, there was created—within the illusion—that called the past and the present and the future; that is, we resided in the present moment, while we still resided in the moment-past and the moment-about-to-become. We stretched time...and all else proceeded within the participation, within the forming of physicality in a way that supported those who resided within it; physicality, supporting the manifesting of beings and then their manifesting, their playing within the moment, the discovery of time.

So now here we are, residing in this moment and we can easily remember what occurred in the previous moment, and we can perhaps project what will occur in the next moment; that is, that I, Teacher, will continue speaking with you, the words that we agreed upon long long ago. Time. Time and our stretching it one way and then another, until we placed ourselves within the moving illusion that said we were, we are and we might be. Not right nor wrong. Just illusionary.

So then in this illusion within stretched time, you and I are going to flow forth and observe the projected future. And because we are not going to be observing the next moment, but are going to be observing the further future, we are asking of ourselves to remain objective and to not react or interpret. We are choosing together to not influence or be influenced; all of which resides within interpretation. I ask you now to determine that you will participate in this manner, for your own benefit and for the benefit of what we are doing together.

This is the moment—the ever present moment—that we are journeying within, my dears. Right here and right now.

SPEAKING SEVEN

In this speaking we are going to bring our awareness closer and closer to the time stream, until we can actually look right into that location where the light is very bright.

invite you to use your imagination. It is well-developed and able to participate easily with what we are about to do. So then, just imagine that we are together, residing in the ethers. What does that mean? How can you imagine that? In this way.

Imagine that we are residing in a way that we are separate from earth, separate from the usual physicality, and that we are together...just being. I am certain that you can accomplish this. You have imagined that you are floating, you have imagined that you are above the clouds, that you are free from whatever is calling to you, free from demands; and now you are simply imagining that you are away from earth itself and that you and I are floating in the ethers.

Just take a moment and close your eyes and imagine what I have described. Take your time, breathe deeply and slip right into that imagining. Don't proceed until you have done that.

Next, we are going to view the time stream together. It is a white flowing, as if a long essence, white in nature, and it is just there beneath us. We don't actually see any movement, we are just looking at what might be a long white tunnel, but we are viewing the outside. Just let that vision form for you. Again, take your time and imagine it. That is really the best way.

Good. Now we are going to bring our viewing closer. You can imagine that there, on the white form there is a bright light shining, brighter than any other location on the tunnel. And as we perceive that white, we decide to move closer and examine what it is, what is causing that light to be brighter than the rest. Just take your time and imagine that light, noticing that light.

And now we are going to bring our awareness closer and closer until we can actually look right into that location where the light is very bright. And as we view into the location on the time stream, we can see that there is something occurring. What is it? Ask yourself, what is occurring and allow the vision, the imagination to view what is occurring in that location.

Remain objective and perceive if there are people, creatures, nature, anything? If you seem to not be able to do this, simply tell yourself or that part of

yourself that holds the belief that you cannot participate in this manner, tell that belief that you have received its message and to be released from you. Then
proceed to view.

You are choosing to participate in this manner, in
this way that will clear away prohibitive beliefs and
efforts that believe they must flow through known
parameters.

Remember this is your imagination and you are in
charge. What does that mean? It means that you are
choosing to participate in this manner, in this way
that will clear away prohibitive beliefs and efforts
that believe they must flow through known parameters. You are simply imagining as you choose and if
there comes a block or a seeming inability, you are
easily just pushing it aside, dissolving it, or ignoring
it. Because you are in charge.

Now view once again that location of the time
stream. You might begin to observe different loca-
tions moving, as if one location is present, and then
another and then another. That is because within the
time stream there is movement, the movement within the stretching of itself, the stretching of time.

Ask the movement to slow so that you can perceive what is occurring. And I will tell you what we
are observing. This first light that we are journeying

to is the exact moment when we all began to become aware of what we might do together, one day, one moment, one blink within the time stream. That is what the light is all about. You might not see human beings or a gathering of beings simply because we were all in spirit form during this moment. Yet together we did breathe this choice into the stretched and moving time stream.

Now just take a deep breath and allow that light to fill you. You are not affecting the time stream in any way, you are simply receiving the frequencies of your very own beingness during the moment of choice, during the moment of decision to proceed in the manner in which we are currently proceeding. Then just allow that truth to fill you.

The light is flowing within you simply because it is of you. It is of the you who is consciously aware and knowing of the truth of being.

You are not causing the filling, you are allowing. And the light is flowing within you simply because it is of you. It is of the you who is consciously aware and knowing of the truth of being. And while you are allowing this to occur, I will speak with you of truth and what we are doing together.

Being conscious of truth while incarnate seems to be an action, yet it is different. This action is a not-doing, a not-reacting, a not-efforting to make something occur. This seeming action is actually a choice, a decision; and the decision is to let go of the efforting that has been occurring in your life.

Now you might be in the midst of creating a new project and you are asking of yourself to remain focused and to create according to your plan. And this new manner of being is asking you to let go a bit. In fact, it is asking you to let go totally and allow. Now you might be tempted to say, "Sure I'll let go and see if anything gets done." Stay with me and I'll explain further.

I am asking you to let go for a moment and allow, allow that real you to come forth, to fill the present moment, and to be-come.

I am not asking you to give up on your project. What I am asking you or inviting you to do is to let go for a moment and allow, allowing that real you to come forth, to fill the present moment, and to be-come. Now to be-come means to set aside your human nature, to set aside your persona, and to flow yourself forth into the moment. How do you flow yourself forth?

This might be the easiest non-action that you do!

You are simply removing your conscious participation with anything and placing your consciousness within, inside, deep within the spirit of your being, where resides the one, the spark of creation. the light of lights, truth.

You are not making that happen. You already exist, always. The real you is always. And you are simply choosing to part the seas of illusion that says that you are human, that you are your body, that you are the persona through which you have been experiencing the journey. You are setting aside all of that and you are remembering.

You are remembering that you are truth, that you are light, that you are I Am. And that all else is nothing. Nothing. Now this truth does not negate all that you have been accomplishing in your project or in your lifely journey. It simply says that the real you is all that there is. Divine.

Now the mind wants to play with that a bit, but just hold off on that and stay with me. Later you can think about it—or not.

You are truth, you are light, you are I Am.

So then, as you let go of considering your project, of thinking about what you will do next, of considering what will work and what won't work; as you let go of participating with all of that and you begin to reside with your consciousness right here in this moment, right here and right how; you are then beginning to allow...to allow your consciousness to flow forth into the truth of who you are. And the strange thing is that you cannot make this happen.

This journey and union is the only yearning that has ever been.

All you can do is, for a moment, stop your busyness and simply be. Refuse your mind's passion to try to figure things out. Just be. And then allow your consciousness to follow its naturally magnetized flowing to truth, to the truth of who you really are. This journey and union is the only yearning that has ever been; all else, all other yearning is an interpretation of this moment, this return of your consciousness to the One, to that which you are, the real you.

Then breathe deeply and allow, while I continue speaking with you.

The time stream flows forth within the creation of itself; and within the time stream, there resides the moment wherein the battle is no more, where there is only truth, where all consciousness is one.

The time stream flows forth within the creation of itself; and within the time stream, there resides the moment wherein the battle is no more, where there is only truth, where all consciousness is one. We have a tendency to think that moment is waaay in the future somewhere, but that moment is the one constant in the time stream. It is always present, and though it resides in the moment past and in the possible next moment, it always is. Why?

Truth. Truth is. Wholeness of being is just that: all one. No separation. Only being one being. That that is the moment—the ever present moment—that we are journeying within, my dears. Right here and right now.

Now it may seem that I have led you around and around, but I have not. As I am speaking in this manner, the words are radiating frequencies that match those within your being, so that you are more and more in the present moment and that you are more and more who you really are, letting go of the assuming of who you might be or might become. You have heard the words again and again. This is all there is. This moment.

Yet, as you can perhaps think, there is so much going on, so much occurring upon the earth, within the cause and effect of each and every one of its inhabitants, including the creatures and earth itself. So much occurring.

And what we are learning how to do together is to reside with that goings-on and not be trapped within it, and not be attached emotionally, and to not be mesmerized by the illusion. And instead…what? We are being who we really are, together, one being, and we are going forth as we planned long long ago.

And I will speak of that going forth in our next step together. But for now, allow yourself to reside in this moment, together, righter here and right now, one being, all who receive these words…one being… you and Teacher, one being.

We are being who we really are, together, one being, and we are going forth as we planned long long ago.

SPEAKING EIGHT

I want you to be able to continue in your lifely journey
free of the attachments that lash out of the insanity,
trying to bring you back into the fold of the sleeping
masses.

n this speaking I am going to teach you. As you have been awakening, you have delighted in new awareness and then continued in your journey. Of course. Yet now is a different time, for you and upon earth. And we have spoken of the insanity that is occurring, deliberately in some instances and in other instances by the participation of the sleeping masses.

I want you to be able to go forth, in your day, whether you enter the masses or remain alone.

I want you to be able to live in a way that refuses to allow that insanity to enter your being, not even for one moment.

I want you to be able to continue in your lifely journey free of the attachments that lash out of the insanity, trying to bring you back into the fold of the sleeping masses.

I want you to be able to live free of your own fears that rest within the foundation of survival.

I want you to be who you really are, incarnate, and filled to the brim and overflowing with your own light, your own inner knowing; so that wherever you are and whomever you are with, you will be free and unaffected.

Oh I want so much for you! So then let's begin learning about how to go forth in this manner, shall we?

Of course you know this all begins with consciousness. Now if you aren't accustomed to that word, then you have perhaps wondered if this teaching is for you. It's just a word, you know. In the context of this teaching of how to go forth within the insanity and not of it, consciousness refers to several things. The first is that you are conscious or awake.

We are speaking of you, the real you, the divine essence which is taking form within that vessel. You.

To be conscious or awake in the context of this teaching, you are simply remembering that you have done nothing wrong and are not atoning for anything, whether it is in this life or a previous life. Now some could debate that and bring up the topic of karma. But I am here to tell you. We met long ago and you were then free from any cause-and-effect poison and you are free of it now. Of course you might have done some things you regret, but that is all part of residing as a human. We are not speaking of your human, your vessel. We are speaking of you, the real you, the divine essence which is taking form within that vessel. You.

The second context of consciousness with regard to this teaching refers to truth, the truth that you are always awakening to the more. What does that mean? It means this. You are here to awaken. And to continue in that process. Even though you are awake or aware of many spiritual truths, still...because you are incarnate, you will continue to awaken. This, of course, is a good thing. It is part of the nourishment of your entire beingness, including your human nature.

And the third context of consciousness with regard to this teaching refers to frequencies. When you choose to bring your mind to right here and right now and refuse to think about anything else, any person, place or situation separate from the now, then you are residing in a way, a manner that allows the frequencies of your inner being to flow forth and be as present as they possibly can be. And along with the words that I am speaking with you, words that are imbued with frequencies designed to assist you, you are then more and more awake and conscious.

So you see? There is really nothing mysterious about the word *consciousness* or its meaning.

This teaching is designed specifically for you.

Then let's get aboard this journey! I'd like to speak a little about what we will be doing, but while I am speaking, I'd also like you to begin to enter into a more expanded-consciousness state; that is, to breathe deeply and let go of your need to focus on anything but right here and right now and what I am saying. Just as if you are entering into a peaceful state, perhaps meditative state.

So, go ahead and do that and I will begin to speak this teaching designed specifically for you.

In the very center of your being, the core of that which you are, there resides a portal. The portal can be opened easily and when it does open, it reveals the truth of who you are. Yet if the portal were to open to one who is not conscious, or awake, then nothing is revealed. This manner has been created long ago as a safeguard against those who are adept at entering the frequencies of beings and accessing their innocence as part of a harvesting of those frequencies that can fuel anything—physical, mental or of spirit. *Rest assured that the portal within your being is intact. And that is one of the reasons that you can receive this teaching.*

Now we are going to journey to that portal, together, and call it to open and to reveal to you the more of who you are. And before you allow yourself to be concerned that you will not be able to do this simply because you have never done it before, just relax in the knowing that none of you have done this before, none of those who are receiving this teaching have done this before.

So, here we go!

Now remember, you are just relaxing into that peaceful way, not letting your mind get busy about anything else. Take some deep breaths and just receive these words, words that hold the frequencies that we designed together long long ago.

The core of creation breathes forth the spark which ignites the forming and unforming.

From the core of creation flows forth what has been called *the All.*

The All flows forth to take form as everything, journeying forth to experience itself in every manner possible.

One of the manners possible is physicality and

all that resides within physicality.

That same portal, that same spark, that same flowing forth, that same All then does reside within you, as you. The All—or divine essence—taking form within physicality as a being, as you.

That means that within your very being resides the core of creation, which allows your residing to be. And this core of creation is what lives behind the portal of which we have spoken.

Within your very being resides the core of creation, which allows your residing to be.

Now there is not a magic word to open the portal, there is nothing that you must do to access the truth of who you are. And I am certain that brings up a puzzling thought. But just let that thought go by and continue to hear my words. Take a few deep breaths and find that peaceful state once again. And I will continue.

The reason that you don't have to do anything to open the portal and access the truth of who you are, the core of creation, is this. You are already it. If it is who you really are, then what else must you do to be who you really are? Nothing.

What we are doing together then, is letting go.

Now this is more than the letting go that you have been doing in your spiritual journey, the journey that has successfully bought you to this moment.

What we are together letting go of—temporarily—is the belief that you are your human nature, that you are the person through which the human travels, and that you are less than divine. Now being divine doesn't mean that you are going to feed your ego. This is way beyond that. You are way beyond that....you were lifetimes ago.

Do then, take another deep breath and refresh your peaceful state, letting go of thoughts about anything and just being right here and right now.

Now I am going to increase our vibrational frequencies together while I invite you to think of yourself as peace, the restful state that you enjoy. Just allow that concept to live with you. You are peace itself.

Feel what that feels like. Peace. Nothing that pulls you to it or repels you from it. Peace. Just being.

Peace is the ability to merge with everything, but yet merging isn't necessary simply because you are the All and the All takes form as everything.

Now I'd like you to know that when you reside

as peace, you are automatically inside the real you, that you have bypassed the portal and you are residing in truth, truth itself. And peace has been and will always be the avenue to the truth of who you really are.

Peace is the ability to merge with everything, but yet merging isn't necessary simply because you are the All and the All takes form as everything.

Now I'm not talking about peace adverse to war. I'm not really talking about physicality at all. I am directing this teaching to the real you, the essence that forms itself incarnate.

Now your mind has never really been able to grasp any of this and the reason is that it is not for the mind. So you can forgive your mind for not understanding all of what I am asking you to experience. In fact, resting in peace gives your mind a vacation for its usual activities.

Now the spark of creation that creates All is the very same spark of creation that resides incarnate as you. AS you. I know, I know that is illusive. But that's where we are right now in this teaching. Just stay with me.

Because the real you is divine essence flowing forth as and from the spark of creation, you are able to reside in the illusion, or distortion of survival, simply because within that distortion and survival, there is the same spark of creation. It is just that the vessels of that spark are asleep and some are steeped in survival's grasp and believe that they have the right to destroy. Yet. Yes, I am saying "yet" because right now I am asking you to let go of focusing on that. I am asking you to continue to remember who you really are.

Do you have it? Within the core of your being—now this isn't within the core of your physicality. We are beyond physicality and are now residing as frequencies. So, within the core of your being does there be the pulse beat of taking form and releasing form, which continually occurs. It is the pulse beat of creation.

Perhaps you will rest within those words for a moment.

Now let's speak about going forth into the fray. How do you best do that and remain free from the magnetic effects, the density of depression, anger, fear, hopelessness. How do you go forth and not be affected? That is what this is all about. This is how you leave the insanity behind.

Firstly, each and every day, bring yourself to that peaceful state of being and then reside within the core of creation that lives in the center of your beingness. Remember, there is no struggle in doing this. You already are what you are determining to reside within. Remember too, that you are simply letting go of identifying yourself as the human and its persona. For this purpose, you are letting go and being as essence itself.

Secondly, breathe your breath. Because you are incarnate, you breathe a breath and within that action are you determining to reside incarnate. As you reside incarnate, cause yourself to remember your purpose set long long ago.

That purpose is to reside awake incarnate and to reside in truth, the truth of who you really are, and then to go forth in that truth and not be magnetized to anything that would pull you off-balance from that inner knowing.

Now sometimes you might be pulled off-balance. That is all right. It isn't a crime. How you can get back in the groove is simple. Just take those deep breaths and rest, remember all that we have been saying, and let go of any need for anything. Proceed with a little scan to see if you have entered into judgment or interpretation. If you have, then let all of that go and return to objectivity. The more that you practice in this way, the more you will be able to go forth free and clear.

Now here is the fulfillment. During your day—
or week if daily is too much for you, and if it is,
that's ok—bring your awareness to the top of your
head, your crown chakra energy center. Just bring
your attention there and then notice a spinning in
that area. Then as if guiding the frequencies of that
spinning downward, invite it to flow all the way
through your entire being and into your feet.

Next, determine to anchor that frequency in your
feet. How do you do that? Easy. Atop your feet is
an energy center in each foot. Bring your awareness
there and cause the center or vortex to spin clock-
wise. Now if you have never done this before, do not
be concerned or frustrated. Just decide that is what
you are causing to happen...and it will happen.

Next, from the very core of your being—inside
the real you—breathe forth that Light of lights, that
Truth of truths. Remember, when you determine
that you will do this, then all follows your determi-
nation...because you are residing in peace. That is
the key. Always reside within peace.

*You are residing in peace. That is the key. Always reside
within peace.*

Just decide that you will take a deep breath and

when you exhale, you will be exhaling the Light of lights, the Truth of truths, the awakened consciousness, that it flow forth into the All. Continue in this manner for eight breathings. Then pause for a moment, and then say the words: So be it.

Now initially you might not feel anything, but I am here to tell you that the more that you *sincerely* participate in this manner, holding peace and breathing forth Light and Truth; the more that you will begin to reside right in the center of what you are doing. There will be no wondering if it is real, there will be no concern for whether you are actually doing it. You will feel yourself right in the presence...the presence of that divine essence which is the real you.

Now perhaps you can glean what I am saying. Keep doing this! Do it once, twice, more than twice. Do it hundreds of times. Do not stop. Participate in this manner as often as you can. It only takes a few moments.

Remember! You are then participating in a way that you determined long long ago, when we came upon this projected future and determined that we would participate in a way that would assist in the awakening and assist in the dissolving of survival's grasp upon the innocence of the sleeping masses.

THIS is what we are doing together. No small potatoes, as you say.

Nature will assist you to balance and align yourself so that you can continue within this purpose easily.

And after you proceed in this manner a few times, I ask you to go into nature and proceed in the same manner. Nature will assist you to balance and align yourself so that you can continue within this purpose easily. While you proceed in this manner in nature, allow yourself to receive also that which you are breathing forth, as if the frequencies go forth, go outward, and then return to you. Do this only when you are in nature.

This then is the participation and incarnating of the divine taking of form and releasing of form. As you breathe outward Truth and Light, *it does take form*. And as it returns to you—when you are in nature—it is the releasing of form and the returning to One. You are then incarnating the Return to One, that which always occurs, yet now you are bringing it into consciousness.

Do you now see? Do you now have a glimpse of the magnitude of what we are doing together? So much more could be in description of the effects, the results of what we do together; yet to remain in the moment of participation is the most important factor. All else becomes history as the previous moment.

Then, my dears, I will release you to or participation. Know that I will be with you always and assist to hold you within the truth of who you really are.

I care deeply for you.

You are then incarnating the Return to One, that which always occurs, yet now you are bringing it into consciousness.

Though there are many many instances of the opposite occurring upon earth, still, the beings and gatherings of light are major and make a major difference in holding at bay the darkness that so very much wants to cover the entire earth.

SPEAKING NINE

I want you to be able to experience yourself in the fullness of truth, in the fullness of who you really are, and in the fullness of the freedom to let go of that which you are not.

What is the insanity? And perhaps a further question might be, how am I contributing to it? And, how can I hold my purpose and still reside incarnate, where everything seems to be increasing in its horrific state?

That's what we are all about here. Now I want to speak with you directly about what is occurring upon earth. Yes, firstly we will agree that there are many gatherings of light beings, many gatherings where beings are holding the light either through meditation, prayer, or residing in a way that holds truth. Now this isn't insignificant. And though there are many many instances of the opposite occurring upon earth, still, these beings and these gatherings of light are major and make a major difference in holding at bay the darkness that so very much wants to cover the entire earth.

Now that is perhaps a frightening statement. It is true, yet I am not speaking these words to illicit fear; more so, I am speaking to you in this manner so that you can understand why it is so very necessary for you to reside in a way that allows you to be who you really are.

So then this speaking flows forth in two phases. Firstly, is the understanding of the darkness that resides upon the earth.

And secondly, I want to be sure that you know how to refuse to reside in the illusionary description of your own self, so that you can more and more enjoy the freedom of being who you are in every circumstance, in every breath, in every pulse beat.

That is to say clearly, I want you to be able to experience yourself in the fullness of truth, in the fullness of who you really are, and in the fullness of the freedom to let go of that which you are not. Then, let's begin!

In understanding the darkness that is so very evident upon earth, you are asking yourself to remain objective. This is an important manner of being. Remaining objective means that you are not entering into a judgment against what we are about to explore.

Now the words might seem easy enough, to remain objective and not judgmental. However, there will be the temptation to judge.

Why don't we want to judge? You will recognize this statement easy enough because it is familiar to you. If you are entering into judgment, you are also entering into the belief of separation from the whole. And that belief is a primary factor in the sleep state. And, my dears, we do want to remain awake.

You see, the sleep state doesn't mean that you don't recognize what is occurring. It doesn't mean that you are putting your head in the sand. And it doesn't mean that you are careless or uncaring.

In this instance, the sleep state means that within your judging, you are then entering into a most painful manner of being. You are, perhaps without realizing, entering into the feeling of being lost. And that feeling of being lost, unconnected to the whole, leads all beings to want to rearrange the external world to give to them the feeling of wholeness. Yet, of course you realize, that feeling cannot be fulfilled in any external rearranging.

So then, when you feel yourself edging toward judgment of any person, place or situation, just take a deep breath and detach. Just let go of entering into the fray of the battle. Again, letting go does not mean that you do not care. Contrarily, it means that you care enough to refuse to increase the frequencies of that which you abhor by not judging, which delivers to that which you are judging the energies of your very own self.

Do you see? When you judge, when you point your finger—perhaps rightfully so—you are then sending your frequencies, your precious frequencies into the battle. And, my dear ones, the battle is the sleep state fully and completely. It is suffering and despair. Perhaps you will reflect upon this for a moment.

Now let's get to speaking about what is occurring upon earth so that you will understand the cause and effect of that battle.

Yes, it is a battle of truth and untruth. It is the age-old battle that has been going on for more than your concept of time. Yet it is here and it is now. As I have spoken, in the past there have been great beings, beings who could hold totality within their consciousness while incarnate. And those beings did go forth and battle. Some in actual battle, others in a way that nourished the whole and diminished the untruth. Now there is not one being. There are many. And of course, you are part of the many who go forth within the pulse beat, within the moment, and are able to hold truth. And we will speak of that and the reality of who you are in the second phase of this teaching.

Now I invite you to take a deep breath and cause yourself to be peaceful, and then I will continue.

The battle that is occurring upon earth in subtle and overt ways, delivers to the masses a false sense of hope while at the same time, harvests their suffering and despair. How does this occur?

When there is a carrot placed before a suffering being and the carrot says that everything will be better if you have this carrot, the suffering being will most likely reach for that carrot. If the being has reached for that carrot several times and found it to be false and unfulfilling, perhaps even detrimental; then there is a bigger carrot offered.

This process continues on and on. The ones who are offering the carrot are those who desire to remain in control of the masses. You see, the more that the masses reach for the carrot and forget what is actually occurring in the cause and effect of their own lives, the more that those in control can harvest their frequencies. Now what does that mean, *harvest their frequencies*? It means this.

When beings are suffering, when beings are filled with despair, when beings reach for something that feels like it might be hope-fulfilled; there is emitted from the very essence of who they are, a frequency.

The frequency is an essence that is of their own life force. That frequency, that essence, flows forth to unite with what might be hope-fulfilled. This is natural. The flowing forth of the life essence fulfills its purpose by uniting with the whole in every circumstance.

Now. Here is the rest of that occurrence. As those who are in control reap the benefits of the suffering of the sleeping masses, they too are reaping the illusion of separation from the whole. They too, then, are hungry for more. They will always be hungry for more and more simply because they—like the sleeping masses—are empty of the consciousness of the whole. Do you see?

Both the sleeping suffering masses and those who are in control are feeding each other with the false hope of fulfillment, when in truth the fulfillment resides in the awakening to truth, the truth that is known within you and within all light beings: all beings are one being. All beings are breathing the same breath. All beings are residing within the same pulse beat. And, all beings are the divine essence flowing forth to take form as everything and everyone. One.

All beings are breathing the same breath. All beings are residing within the same pulse beat. And, all beings are the divine essence flowing forth to take form as everything and everyone. One.

Within the sleep state, that truth is most diffi-
cult to even comprehend, never mind accept. Why?
Because, my dears, there is a learned attachment to
the persona, to the belief that who they are creating
themselves to be is the real self. Yet within that belief,
there resides emptiness. I am certain you can bring
your own consciousness to this truth. Right here and
right now.

The persona, beautiful as it may be, is simply the
vessel for the human nature, a manner for the human
nature to experience its journey. Yet, I repeat myself
in saying that both the human nature and its persona
are but vessels.

They are your vessels, along with your body-physical, and they allow you to reside incarnate and to
continue to awaken to the truth of who you are. That
is really all the awakening is about. You are continually given the opportunity to recognize who you are.
Perhaps you can understand this more clearly if I say
that you are continually given the opportunities to
recognize who you are not.

So then, as the darkness or sleep state continues
to grow upon the earth, there then resides a force. It
is a force of destruction. And its purpose is to destroy, dissolve, and cause to be no more, those factors
of truth, those manners of being that celebrate the

wholeness of being, those manners of residing that celebrate the truth that all beings are one being. The darkness and its frequencies cannot bear to awaken. They are too invested in their control and the illusion of being better than any whom they control.

Now is the time to be sure that you are not entering into judgment, my dears.

In the entire picture of this battle upon earth, there is the recognizing that battle is futile, yet it continues. Many many beings are delivering their suffering and their body-physical, their life force, to the cause of the battle; believing that they are entering into an honorable cause.

You might be asking, "If we do not battle, then those in control will cause more suffering, more slaughter, more darkness." And you would be right in those thoughts. And I say this to you: hear my words.

There are those who have incarnated upon earth, those who are war mongers of old. There are those who are of the light who have taken to themselves the cause of the battle. To do so has been a monumental sacrifice; yet they are proceeding in this manner. They, those ancient warriors of old, are entering into the battle.

You who receive these words are not ancient warriors of old. You are here, as I have spoken, to hold and anchor the light of truth…yes, while the battles continue. Why? How can you be helping the battle?

You are not helping the battle. No one will win the battle. Yet when the battle ceases to be, then all beings will be one being. All beings will be Home. All beings will know truth, light, love and …yes, peace, inner peace wherein there resides nourishment of the spirit.

No one will win the battle. Yet when the battle ceases to be, then all beings will be one being. All beings will be Home. All beings will know truth, light, love and …yes, peace, inner peace wherein there resides nourishment of the spirit.

Now I will speak about how you can reside in the truth of who you are and to let go of that which you are not, all while journeying through the cause and effect wherein resides the battle and the frequencies of the battle. This is called leaving the insanity behind.

Again I say, this manner of being does not mean that you are uncaring. It does mean that you care so very much that you are dedicated to fulfilling your purpose. You are dedicated to residing in the joy and peace of your own beingness, the truth of who you are.

For every moment that you reside in this manner—

and I am going to teach you more about how to reside in this manner—the more that the awakening flows forth, the more that all beings are embraced in the essence of truth, the essence of light, and the essence of the divine breath of creation itself. Flowery words? Not really. Truth? You betcha.

Now let's begin with the basic concept of who you are. Well, it's not that basic. You are able to receive it because you are awake.

As you reside incarnate, there radiates from you great light, great truth. Truth is a vibrational frequency; it is not a gathering of words in a book or encyclopedia. It is a frequency.

So then, when you are residing as you are, knowing that you are a divine essence that resides within all of the vessels we have been speaking about: the body-physical, the human nature and its persona; when you reside within this knowing, you are then automatically radiating truth, radiating light, radiating love.

Now that might be a wonderful truth for you to know.

So then the trick of it all is to be able to maintain that knowing of who you really are. Some beings have used words to remind them of this truth, the truth that they are divine essence incarnate. Some beings have meditated and brought their awareness to the present moment, within which they hold their breath of creation. Some call this mindfulness.

And other beings have discovered different ways of bringing their consciousness into the present moment, remembering the truth of who they are, then being able to carry that truth, that consciousness with them wherever they journey, even into the fray of the battle, even into the illusion of separation form the whole.

So then, how can you proceed in that manner and why would you want to? You might have a slight wondering of "what's in it for me? Why do I want to dedicate my energies toward this manner?" And don't be embarrassed if you have those thoughts, even if they are subtle. The subtlety might present itself as, "I don't have time for this." Or, "My life is too busy for this." Those thoughts are not a crime either. They are natural. Why?

Those thoughts are the mind's way of trying to keep you "as you are". And why would the mind want that? Because the unknown is something that the mind cannot control. This is beyond the mind, my dears. Beyond everything. It is leaving the insanity behind. Ready?

Here we go!

Perhaps the real question is, how can I experience

who I truly am? And here is the answer. Begin in this way. Begin by setting aside your connection to your body. What do I mean by that? This.

Even though you might not realize it, your perception of who you are is very much connected to your body-physical. That is, if you reside within a healthy body, your perception of who you are is strong. If you reside in a body that is not up to the standards of what you see in your programming, then your perception of who you are is not as strong. You believe that you must do something to get to be the image of perfection, of the best body-physical.

Some actually believe that they are not a real being until they can make their body-physical the way it is supposed to be, whether that is losing weight, gaining weight, being more active, more limber, more and more. In this instance, you have placed your concept of self in the future somewhere. One day your body will be the way you would like it to be and then, oh then, you will be a real person. Until then, you are just not who you are supposed to be.

Do you see how this back and forth plays with your concept of self? Do you see how you depend on your body-physical to tell you who you are and if you are good enough?

Then why not take this moment to set aside the

concept of what you believe your body should be, or set aside the concept that because your body is what you want it to be, you are a real being as long as you can maintain that body.

Let's set aside your attachment to your body physical, your criticisms of your body, your loving your body. Just set aside living through the condition of your body.

Now remember, you are dealing with an attachment. It might be quite strong. It is either negative or positive, but you have been focused on your body in a way that has not allowed you to go beyond the physical. The physical has become your sense of self.

Then take a deep breath and simply decide. Perhaps you will say these words, *"I am deliberately setting aside my attachment to my body's condition to tell me who I am."* You might have your own words, but those will suffice for the moment. Perhaps this is a little awakening for you. If so, then bravo!

Next, let's set aside the persona. Yes, the character you have developed and believe is who you are. It is not. It is simply a vehicle for your human nature to experience this journey. You might have developed a lovely character, or persona. But just set that aside, as if you are removing a hat, just lift it off of your being and set it aside. Take a moment to do this.

Next and lastly, set aside your concept that you are

a human being. You are living inside the vessel of a human being so that you can be incarnate, but you are not a human being. You can know this to be true because you have observed your human being or human nature's tendencies and wondered at the why of certain actions. And as many teachers have then taught by asking *who is observing*, I, too, encourage you to set aside your experiencing through your human nature. This is easy because we are simply being in this moment.

What remains? Divine Essence. The whole. All that is. You. The real you without the need to be somebody. Now I ask you to breathe deeply and simply reside in this moment. Bring your awareness within your being. You are letting go of your body, your human nature, your character or persona, and you are right inside this moment. You, for this moment, have no vessels. You have set them aside.

You are pure essence of being. The divine. You might require yourself to practice this manner of being; that is, you might want to practice several times, letting go of all that I have guided you to do.

When you are no longer asking your body to tell you if you are all right, when you are no longer asking your character or persona to act a certain way to give you stability in your lifely journey, and when you are no longer viewing yourself as your human nature vessel, what is left? What is left is the real you.

I do so very much wish you to experience this real you. In a manner of speaking you do not have to effort to experience who you really are. You, the divine essence, always is. You might say that once you set aside all of your vessels, you are allowing, allowing your conscious knowing to be.

Now you might find this a bit illusive and that would be because you are trying to experience all of this through your mind. But remember, your mind cannot explore the divine simply because your mind is filled with parameters through which this knowing must travel. Then set aside your thinking about all of this. What I am asking you to do is to reside in this moment, right here and right now.

Your mind cannot explore the divine simply because your mind is filled with parameters through which this knowing must travel.

Breathe deeply.

Set aside all of those vessels.

Set aside trying to think about what you are being asked to explore.

Just tell your mind that you will think about it all

later, after you have experienced what we are doing together.

And just be. Allow. Allow the divine essence that is the real you to be…you. Allow your consciousness to expand to include the whole. You are simply allowing and not trying to figure out how to do all of this. You are not doing. You are being.

Just remain in this manner for as long as you can. Your mind will eventually take over and that is all right. Yet when you return to this simply because you cannot stay away from the essence, the divine essence that is you, your mind will begin to respect this choice and allow you longer and longer to be.

This is the first requirement to leaving the insanity behind, even as you journey through it.

I invite you to practice or participate in this manner until you can truly recognize the difference between the vessels and the real you. You can do this, my dears. It is like shedding winter clothing on a hot summer's day.

Next I will speak about journeying through the insanity and not being part of it, not being taken into its fold, but remaining free and at the same time fulfilling your purpose. Oh, you are going to like this!

Letting go does not mean that you do not care. Contrarily, it means that you care enough to refuse to increase the frequencies of that which you abhor by not judging, which delivers to that which you are judging the energies of your very own self.

SPEAKING TEN

This freedom is your real journey, your real residing. This freedom is the dance you have been waiting for. Freedom. This is your real invitation to leave the insanity behind.

Now we are going to go forth, holding the truth of who we really are, and enter into the fray of the insanity. You won't have to look for the insanity. The sleep state is all about you. Just as the light and truth state is all about you. Now that should give you some clue to how we will proceed.

When you enter into the insanity, you are actually, with each stepping, parting the seas of the untruth.

Don't worry that you won't be able to hold in your consciousness the truth of who you really are. Why? Because you are always who you really are. It is natural to bounce back and forth. That is, once you have discovered the real peace within your being, the real you, it will feel so very wonderful that it will be easy to reclaim your conscious awareness.

For example, I am asking you to breathe deeply and bring yourself to the awareness that you have been recognizing as the real you. Don't be in a hurry. Just take your time, breathe deeply, pause and remember who you are not.

You are not your vessels. Yes, you appreciate them as you will go forth using all three—your body-physical, your human nature and its persona –but inside, deep inside your being lives that divine essence which you can always experience as peace.

So then, fill yourself with that peace. And when you are ready, go forth into the fray. Now going forth into the fray might be as simple as journeying where there is the populace, perhaps even in a mall. As you enter the fray or the gathering of beings who are going about their own journey, pause for a moment and feel. Feel the energies.

What do you feel? You feel the confusion, the flowing of efforting, the flowing of trying hard to be something, get somewhere, know something...all to find that carrot and grab on to it.

Now you are still maintaining the knowing of your inner peace, yet you are also becoming aware of the sleeps state. The sleep state is not sleepy; it is harried energies that will not merge into peace because they cannot...yet.

Perhaps you will simply observe beings as they go about their own journey. And perhaps every once in a while you will observe a being who is at peace, who might look your way and smile simply because he or she recognizes the light that you are emanating and that light is a match to their own.

It doesn't mean that you hold the same beliefs or priorities. This is something bigger. It does mean that you are both knowing that you are but one being, going forth to explore the journey of the many. And when you nod or smile back to that being, there is a seeming increase within your own conscious awareness of your inner peace, your inner wholeness of being. Breathe that into your consciousness. Recognize it.

Now when you are going forth in this manner, you are daring to be who you really are and the battle, the sleep state flows about you but not into you. Do you see? It cannot own you because you are no longer ownable. You are awake. And, my dears, you are free.

What happens if you see something, you observe and begin to judge? Perhaps you see some beings who are arguing. Perhaps you see something that reminds you of the horrors of the battle. And when you interpret that viewing as the battle and something you do not want to be a part of, what happens? Notice. Notice that you have briefly let go of your conscious awareness of the real you.

Now that is not a crime, it doesn't mean that you

are lost. It does mean that you are still awake. Why? Because in the moment you recognize what has happened. You feel it. Pay attention to that feeling. And right then and there, when you feel that terrible sickness inside, stop. Stop looking outward at anything. Take a deep breath, close your eyes for a moment, and let go. Let go of whatever caused you to need to find a difference, to find a separation from the fray.

You see, this is the trick of it all. All beings are one being. There is no separation from the whole. There cannot be. Yet. Yes, yet, as beings go forth within the journey, there is that battle, that grasping for the carrot, the external illusionary fulfillment of the inner emptiness. That is the real sleep state.

Now when you, in that moment, find that you need to separate yourself from what has just caused you to judge, you are actually forgetting truth and believing the illusion. Don't begin judging yourself for this. You have been doing it for a very long time, all through your journey to awakening. And now, here you are awake. Then, celebrate.

Celebrate your awareness and the recognizing of that sick feeling inside. In that moment you have succeeded in refusing to enter the sleep state and be lost once again. In that moment, you have chosen to remember who you really are.

Then also in that moment, breathe deeply, let go of everything that has just occurred, bring your focus back to who you really are and remember...remember these words, remember the feeling of inner peace, and remember who you are walking within the fray.

You are walking within the fray to practice, to practice maintaining the truth of who you really are and while you go forth in this manner, you are radiating truth, light and the essence of peace.

Do you see? While you are determining to be who you really are...consciously...you are also fulfilling your purpose.

And all you are doing is practicing remembering, practicing holding your focus on truth and allowing the illusion to pass you by. Now what is the illusion in this instance?

The illusion is the many who have disguised themselves to themselves as lost human beings, searching for the carrot. In truth, they are of the whole, just as are you. They are residing in their journey toward awakening.

And your light, emanating form the core of your being, is like a taping on the shoulder, from somewhere, as if a spirit has tapped them on their shoulder, asking them to remember...remember something. They aren't sure what they are being called to remember, but that is all right. That tapping on the shoulder is part of your divine essence, part of your truth of being, part of your radiating light, which automatically embraced the whole...now hear this...because it is the whole.

So then, here we are now, back to entering the fray and remembering the truth of who you are. My dears, this is just the beginning. You are going to leave the insanity behind...way behind. Now let's be clear about this.

You are not leaving the essence of wholeness of being behind. You are not separating yourselves from those beings who are seeming to be asleep and lost and suffering. Yes, you have compassion for their journey, and yes, you continue to hold to the truth of who you are. What does this mean in your daily life? Does it mean that you stay away from certain beings?

It means this. While you have compassion for all beings who are suffering and caught within the battle, you are not really clear who is of those who would take your frequencies gladly and cause you to forget, cause you to suffer.

Yet, leaving the insanity behind is totally bringing your conscious awareness to truth so very completely that the harvesters of the suffering could tap you on the shoulder and they would never reach the real you.

They would be tapping upon the illusion and such a tapping to the real you, does not even exist. It is as if a breeze that slips away before any recognizing is needed. Do you see?

You care. You love. You perhaps assist beings, some beings. Yet firstly, you are who you are. You have had the saying "you first" and it has carried many different meanings.

This is the most important meaning you can bring to yourself. Always you first. Always bringing your consciousness to truth.

The more that you do this, the more that your thinking mind will be less tempted to view others and judge them as sleeping while you are not.

The mind doesn't know or realize yet that it is, in that moment, participating with the battle in a way that diminishes your conscious knowing of the truth of who you are.

Yet the more that you cause yourself to reside in the very core of your being, to reside deeper and deeper into the inner peace that is your divine knowing, the more that your mind will begin to let go of its need to be the boss. Your mind will begin to enjoy the freedom to play, to reside in the moment.

When you are residing in the moment, remembering the truth of who you are, then you have entered timelessness. And within the timelessness there are no words, no concepts, nothing. And that is when you are residing in the truth of who you are.

Do you see?

Oh you won't really know what I am speaking about until you actually go forth and participate in what I have been teaching you. Participate.

I am asking you to take those moments each day and set aside everything but the moment, breathe deeply and remember that you are not your vessels, and just be…in the moment…truth.

Your mind, as I have said, will want to say something, anything to be part of this practice. But truly, the practice is also setting aside that thinking mind. Just tell your mind that you will think about everything later.

Continue in this practice, my dears and you will be able to easily and completely leave the insanity behind, easily refuse without efforting, refuse the battle and its temptations, refuse the invitation to reach for the carrot, and my dears, you will be free.

This freedom is your real journey, your real residing. This freedom is the dance you have been waiting for. Freedom.

This is your real invitation to leave the insanity behind.

Now once you have practiced in this manner, there is something else waiting for you. It's this.

When you are residing in the moment, remembering the truth of who you are, then you have entered timelessness. And within the timelessness there are no words, no concepts, nothing. And that is when you are residing in the truth of who you are.

SPEAKING ELEVEN

In that moment, when you realize that you don't rightly know what you are excited about, you will be divinely incarnate. That is what you are excited about.

Once you are able to enter into the fray and maintain your conscious knowing of the truth of who you are, then...oh then, my dears, you are free to explore the real journey. What is the real journey? Oh you are going to love this!

The real journey is your fulfillment.

From within your being then, does flow forth those nudgings, those little inklings of something that you have perhaps never considered or something that you long ago considered but set aside as not practical enough, or set aside because it would not make enough money, or set aside because the call into the illusion became as a better invitation.

But now, oh now, you are free of that invitation into the illusion and you are able to recognize that spark, that little feeling of excitement about something.

You might not be able to attach that feeling to

anything. And in that moment, when you realize that you don't rightly know what you are excited about, you will be divinely incarnate. That is what you are excited about.

And within that feeling, that incarnating, resides the freedom to go forth. The going forth in a way that gives to you "the more of who you are" yet can never increase who you are, or diminish who you are.

This journey now gives to you the real moment, the real gift. The gift is that following of one foot, one stepping and then another stepping, until you find yourself doing something that you never really dreamed of doing, but here you are, trying something new, daring to enter into a new project, going to a new class on a topic you hadn't even previously considered, and in those moments, you are residing in your own light, in your own truth. It really doesn't matter what happens next. Why?

Oh my dears, you are the divine essence consciously awake to its own beingness.

Yet know this to be true: whatever you do, you will already be fulfilled even before you begin.

Yes, you will go forth in new ways and perhaps discover new participations upon earth. Yet know this to be true: whatever you do, you will already be fulfilled even before you begin.

Yes, the excitement of your new participating will carry you further within your incarnate journey, and yes it will give to you a sense of real fulfillment. Trust that feeling. It is your real joy. Your real freedom. Your real residing. You. Awake.

And the fray is about you, but it is not. How can that be?

Remember, all is illusion 'cept that which is truth. You have then successfully left the insanity behind. You are real. Very real. You are truth incarnate.

Now for the practicality of it all.

Each day that you go forth in the manner of recognizing who you are, what are your vessels, and refusing to enter into judgment—the portal to suffering—you are daring to clear the way, part the seas, and to find your steppings upon the real earth, the earth of long long ago whereupon truth resided effortlessly. You are residing in the timelessness and that which was of long ago is of the present and you within it.

You might not think this is practical at all, but that is just your mind trying to find a way to relate to that which is bigger than thoughts. That is all right.

Your mind is a good tool, yet before thinking about

anything, there is the real experience and sometimes the experience cannot be described with words.

If you find this to be true, then you are residing in the real thing. And it is there that I am residing with you.

Truth. Light. Love. Embracing the All.

Breathing a breath upon the illusion, simply because you can.

Finding your feet stepping upon the real earth.

Knowing. Inner knowing that you are real, so very real, that you are truth itself, peace itself.

And the battle is no more. Never won, never lost.

Just dissolved into the nothingness.

Yes, in the next moment, there might be a being who presents him- or herself in a way that reminds you of the fray, reminds you of the battle, reminds you of the suffering.

And in that moment, your compassion will rise and you will love…you will love the peace inside that being, the peace that has not yet become conscious.

And your loving will change everything, but you won't know that because you will have continued onward, placing one step after another, enjoying the excitement of truth incarnate consciously celebrating… everything.

I am waiting for you there…here…right here, right

now. You. Free. Just as you have always been…just as you were long long ago in the beginning of time.

One breath, one letting go, one celebrating. Easy. Your path to freedom, leaving the insanity behind. So be it.

❦

Your loving will change everything, but you won't know that because you will have continued onward, placing one step after another, enjoying the excitement of truth incarnate consciously celebrating…everything.

❦

SPEAKING TWELVE
(Addendum)

I have come forth to speak this teaching to you, for you. I am reaching out the hand of love, offering you a rescue, a rescue from succumbing to despair over what resides in the battle, in the suffering.

I am offering you a hand of love and if you dare to take it, you can discover a new freedom and the freedom will give you a way to love, to care and still be free from that aching heart over the suffering of the masses.

My dears, I realize that to some of you, this speaking is a bit illusive. That is all right. You are not behind. There is no such thing as being ahead or being behind. You are simply asking of yourself to dare. To dare to enter into a more expanded knowing of truth.

All of this might not fit into anything that you have ever read before. That is all right too. You might set this book down and wonder why on earth you decided to access this teaching. And that is all right too.

But, my dears, one day you will pick it back up again. Maybe you are sick of the horrific occurrences upon earth and you just don't know how to go forth while the cause and effect continues to be horrible? Then, you will perhaps be ready to find a new way.

Yes, this is a new way, yet it is not new at all. It is simply real. Yes, all of the horribleness is real. It is the battle and within it there is great grave suffering. And yes, you have probably decided that you cannot bear even to hear about it, yet it confronts you each day.

Even when you have decided to refuse to look at the news or read the news, a word here or a conversation there brings it all back.

I have come forth to speak this teaching to you, for you. I am reaching out the hand of love, offering you a rescue, a rescue from succumbing to despair over what resides in the battle, in the suffering.

I am offering you a hand of love and if you dare to take it, you can discover a new freedom and the freedom will give you a way to love, to care and still be free from that aching heart over the suffering of the masses.

Dare you? Give your aching heart a chance to be delivered, to be freed of its own suffering. Give yourself a chance to really live, to really be...be who you are, the real you, able to part the seas of insanity and leave it behind.

This invitation continues…as long as you need it to continue.

Don't wait too long…you needn't suffer any longer.

My love for you is boundless, endless…and real.

Dare you? Give your aching heart a chance to be delivered, to be freed of its own suffering. Give yourself a chance to really live, to really be…be who you are, the real you, able to part the seas of insanity and leave it behind.

ACKNOWLEDGMENTS

This is a special thank you for all who have supported the work that I am gifted to do. I have been blessed to channel classes, deep personal guidance, and daily reflections since the 1980's.

Thank you to Grayson Howell for standing by me...always.

Thank you to Craig Burdett, colleague and friend, for continuing to creatively present my work in artistic and beautiful ways, and for sticking by me when times were rough.

There are many more dear people in my life...you know who you are. I suppose we all have dear ones. I do. I hold you in my heart, where you have always been.

Miriandra

ABOUT THE AUTHOR

Author, lecturer, deep-level channeler, and explorer, Miriandra Rota has been working in the spiritual field for nearly 40 years and is the author and channeler of numerous books and audio programs. Miriandra enjoys assisting people to discover the freedom to explore who they really are, and is dedicated to sharing expanded consciousness truths. She lives with her husband, Grayson Howell, in the mountains of Virginia.

For information about personal sessions, books and audios: www.miriandra.com.

SUGGESTED MEDITATIONS

There are several meditations, varying in depth and purpose, available on my website.

Three Advanced Meditations have been created to assist in deep-level meditation. Here is the web page for all of them: www.miriandra.com/audios/

www.ingramcontent.com/pod-product-compliance
Lightning Source LLC
Chambersburg PA
CBHW070803100426
42742CB00012B/2231